# A Kid's Spring EcoJournal

*With Nature Activities for Exploring the Season*

Toni Albert

*Designed and Illustrated by*
Margaret Brandt

## Trickle Creek Books

"Teaching Kids to Care for the Earth"

Tel: 717-766-2638 • 800-353-2791 • Fax: 717-766-1343
**www.TrickleCreekBooks.com**

W9-BMV-723

## Author's Acknowledgments

Thank you, Bob Albert, for our home at Trickle Creek,
for clearing the land and building the house with your own hands,
for long happy walks in the woods, and long happy days together.

Thank you, Pat Van Etten, for your remarkable friendship and fine work.

Thank you, Margaret, for letting your love of nature
shine through every beautiful page of art.

## Artist's Acknowledgments

I'd like to dedicate this art to the memory of my mother,
and to thank my husband and my father for their unwavering love and support.

A special thanks to Sandra M. Blair for her help in rendering the illustrations
on pages 11, 17, 19, 33, 47, 49, and 54 when we were short of time.

## Dedication

To the vast wildlands and innumerable species of wildlife in the world—
and to the little wildernesses in our backyards.

Copyright © 1997 by Toni Albert
All rights reserved
Printed in the United States of America on recycled paper
First Edition

First printing 1997, Second printing 2005

### Publisher's Cataloging in Publication
(Prepared by Quality Books Inc.)

Albert, Toni.
    A kid's spring ecojournal : with nature activities for
exploring the seasons / Toni Albert; illustrated and designed
by Margaret Brandt.
    p. cm.
    SUMMARY: Includes tips on writing about nature, short
entries from the author's nature journal, and nature activities for
exploring the season.
    Preassigned LCCN: 96-61929
    ISBN-13: 9780964074231
    ISBN-10: 1-9640742-3-0
    1. Nature study—Juvenile literature. 2. Natural history—
Juvenile literature. 3. Ecology—Juvenile literature. 4. Spring—
Juvenile literature. 5. Diaries—Authorship—Juvenile literature.
I. Title.

QH48.A53 1997               574.5'43
        QB197-40028

Published in the United States by Trickle Creek Books
500 Andersontown Road, Mechanicsburg, PA 17055

The purchase of this material entitles the buyer to reproduce
activities for private use or classroom use only—not for commercial
resale. Reproduction of these materials for an entire school or district
is prohibited. Any other use or reproduction of these materials
requires the prior written consent of Trickle Creek Books.

All of the nature activities in this book should be done with
proper supervision from a responsible adult. The publisher is
not responsible for accidents or injuries that may occur when
children explore the natural world.

# Contents

# Introduction
## Writing About Nature

Throughout the ages, writers have been inspired by nature. In springtime, writers have captured every spring experience from the loveliness of cherry blossoms to the noisy chorus of spring peepers in a pond. They have celebrated the excitement of nature starting over and renewing the Earth. You can join the celebration by keeping a spring eco-journal, a personal nature journal.

## What should you write in your eco-journal?
## Anything about nature...

- Write daily notes about the way the season progresses. This takes careful observation. For example, did you ever notice that spring works its way *up* from the ground to the underbrush to the trees?

- Write a poem, a story, or an essay. Draw inspiration from a golden sunrise, a field of wildflowers, or the flight of a hawk. Express your thoughts and feelings about nature.

- Make quick field notes when you are observing something outside. Record details that you may forget later—the colors of a bird, the shape of a flower, the size of a turtle, the pattern on a butterfly. Field notes often include the date and time, the weather, and the location, as well as a description of what you were observing and what happened to it while you were watching. (You can make quick drawings, too.)

- Use your field notes to write a careful description of what you observed. Use detailed, descriptive language.

- Keep a record of an interesting nature study or experiment, such as raising tadpoles, dissecting a bird's nest, or planting a garden.

- Write an interview with a park ranger, a person who has visited a rainforest, a zookeeper, or someone who knows something special about wildlife or wildlands.

- Write a report about an animal or plant that interests you.

- Keep a nature diary with descriptions of special events, such as seeing a red fox run across the road or noticing when a favorite tree blooms.

- Read a book about nature. Then write your response.

- Write a song that a bird might sing.

Keeping an eco-journal will give you a chance to write from your own direct experience. (And writing based on experience is often your best writing.) It is easy to draw inspiration from nature. As you write in your eco-journal, you may find yourself painting word pictures and making your writing sound like poetry. Writing about nature will help you learn to be more observant and to enjoy nature more, too.

# Exploring Nature

It's fun to run through a field of tall grass, scramble up rocks, crash through the underbrush, or splash in a creek. But that's not the best way to see wildlife. You need to learn to enter the quiet world of animals and plants slowly and gently without disturbing them. You must practice being still—but with all your senses alert. You must become observant and more observant and more and more observant! Then you'll see where a robin is nesting and how it pulls a worm from the ground. Or spot a groundhog diving into its burrow. Or see a spider rushing to an insect struggling in its web. It takes patience and skill to explore nature, but the delight of discovery and the joy of caring for our Earth will last all of your life.

## Here are some tips for exploring nature:

- Wear long pants, a long-sleeved shirt, and sturdy shoes. Wear greens and browns.

- Be prepared. Bring drinking water, bug spray, plastic containers for collecting specimens, a magnifying lens, and a notebook and pencil. If you have a camera, binoculars, or field guides, bring them, too. Bring a small trash bag for litter.

- Look for animals at dawn or dusk. That's when you will be most likely to see them.

- Move quietly. Sit still in one place for awhile—at least five minutes. Hide partly behind a tree or boulder. Try to feel like a part of nature.

- Watch where you step (don't step on a snake!) and don't put your hands into hollow logs or trees before you look inside.

- Use all of your senses. Listen to the sounds around you. Breathe deeply and notice different smells. Look around you and observe details. Touch the bark of trees, fuzzy moss, smooth stones in a creek. Taste edible plants and berries *only* when an adult is with you and gives you permission. (Some plants are poisonous.) Don't forget to use your sense of wonder, too!

- Look for signs of wildlife: animal tracks, animal trails, burrows, nests, feathers or fur, bones, droppings, and evidence that animals have eaten or grazed (squirrels drop nutshells, rabbits strip leaves from small plants, birds take berries from bushes).

- If you see an animal and want to get closer, don't approach it directly. Take a roundabout route, walking slowly and steadily. Don't look the animal in the eye or you will alarm it. The best way to get a closer look at an animal is with binoculars.

- If you see a bird, keep your eyes on it until it flies out of sight. Notice its colors and special markings, its shape, and the kind of bill it has. When the bird is gone, make notes of what you saw. Later, you can find it in a field guide to birds.

- Stay on a path or marked trail. Then you won't get lost and you won't trample delicate plants or animal nests.

- Always leave an area as clean as you found it—or cleaner. When you leave, carry trash out with you. Replace any rocks or logs you overturned as you looked for tiny wildlife.

# Spring EcoJournal

Today I looked at a tree. I am going to tri to look at it every day. I can't wait to see it chang.

**March 10:** I live with my husband Bob and our cat Bailey and our dog Abercrombie on twenty acres of wooded land in Pennsylvania. The meadows and trees around our home, the tiny creek that runs through the woods, and a large pond are perfect places for gathering information and inspiration from nature.

Today was cold and snowy. Abercrombie and I walked beside the little creek that we call Trickle Creek. It bubbles up from a spring, flows through the icy pond, and tumbles between snowy banks. As we walked, there was a hushed silence. It was only broken by our feet crunching in the snow and the chuckling of Trickle Creek, which for once is more than a trickle because of the spring thaw.

I looked for signs of spring, but the earth still seems to be sleeping under its white blanket. I wondered if Abercrombie was looking for signs of spring, too. He was certainly busy. He's a small brown dog that can work his way under rose brambles and fallen branches. He loves to take all the secret side trails made by small animals.

As we approached our house, we saw last year's fawns nibbling at some shelled corn that was spread in the driveway for the birds. They watched us for a moment. Then white tails high, they ran into the shelter of the woods. But not very far. Before I had shut the door, the fawns, in their shaggy winter coats, were eating corn again.

© Trickle Creek Books

# Trickle Creek

One of the best ways to learn about nature is to visit the same place over and over until you know it by heart. The place you choose to observe can be your backyard or school yard, a vacant lot or city park, a nature trail or country path, or even a single tree rising above city pavement. For example, if you looked—*really* looked—at the same tree every day for a year, you would learn to know that tree like a friend. You would enjoy every big event in the life of the tree: the appearance of flowers, fruit, seeds, or nuts; a nesting bird; a wind-broken branch; the coloring of leaves in the fall. And you would teach yourself to notice every small change: the loosening of a tightly furled bud, mildew on a leaf, drops of sticky sap attracting insects, squirrel scratches on a branch. The more you get to know about a tree or a trail or your backyard, the more you will care about it. You'll not only become skilled at observing, but you'll be a better conservationist.

It's fun to make a map or drawing—perhaps a view from the air—of the place you choose to observe. You can make notes on your drawing to keep track of seasonal changes, wildlife sightings, and sources of water, food, and shelter for wildlife.

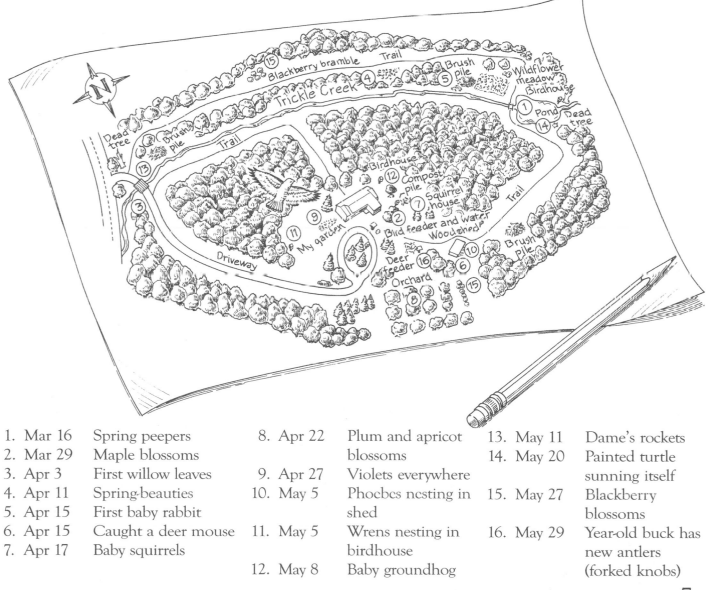

1. Mar 16  Spring peepers
2. Mar 29  Maple blossoms
3. Apr 3  First willow leaves
4. Apr 11  Spring-beauties
5. Apr 15  First baby rabbit
6. Apr 15  Caught a deer mouse
7. Apr 17  Baby squirrels

8. Apr 22  Plum and apricot blossoms
9. Apr 27  Violets everywhere
10. May 5  Phoebes nesting in shed
11. May 5  Wrens nesting in birdhouse
12. May 8  Baby groundhog

13. May 11  Dame's rockets
14. May 20  Painted turtle sunning itself
15. May 27  Blackberry blossoms
16. May 29  Year-old buck has new antlers (forked knobs)

© Trickle Creek Books

# Spring EcoJournal

_____

_____

_____

_____

_____

_____

_____

_____

_____

_____

_____

_____

_____

_____

_____

*March 16:* March is sometimes called "the awakening month." Today I finally saw some signs that the sleepy earth is waking up. Tiny seedlings, which all look alike at this stage, cover the floor of the woods. From a distance, the delicate little plants are only a faint green glow, but, oh! what promise!

There are other signs of spring, too. I heard birdsongs and frog songs. The spring peepers, little brown tree frogs, are presenting a shrill peeper-symphony from the pond. As I stood listening to as much of the noisy concert as I could stand, a pair of mallard ducks landed on the water. It would be wonderful if they decided to nest here.

When we first bought this land sixteen years ago, we asked a forester to explore the woods with us. We told him that we wanted to attract wildlife and provide a good habitat for animals. As he pointed out trees and plants with berries and nuts and buds and seeds, and den trees and brushy cover, and the little creek with fresh, chuckling water, he began to laugh. He said, "This land couldn't be more perfect for wildlife if you had planted every plant yourselves." And he was right. We've enjoyed living in a woods *filled* with wildlife. All we need is a pair of mallards....

8

© Trickle Creek Books

# Save a Place for Wildlife

Wouldn't it be fun to invite all kinds of wildlife to live in your backyard or school yard? You would be able to watch them and learn about them, and at the same time, you would be providing a home for them. You can create a mini-refuge for animals by supplying four things that they need: food, water, cover, and nesting sites.

The ideal way to feed wildlife is to plant trees, shrubs, and grasses that harbor insects and produce nuts, acorns, berries, fruits, and seeds. The right plantings will attract birds and butterflies, squirrels and rabbits, and mice and moles. Of course, you can provide food at feeders, too. Put out sunflower seeds, thistle seeds, millet, corn, and suet.

All animals need water to drink and to bathe in. You can build a little pool or simply set a shallow pan of water on the ground. If you keep the container full of fresh water and set it near a bird feeder, birds will love it. (*See page 43, "Make an Eco-Pond," for more information.*)

Cover for wildlife is any place that protects animals from predators or the weather. Different animals like different kinds of cover. Chipmunks dive into rock piles, rabbits hide in brush piles, squirrels need trees, pheasants like tall grass, and many birds shelter in shrubs. A standing dead tree or a fallen log can provide a home for birds, squirrels, snakes, opossums, raccoons, and skunks. Remember that planting shrubs can do double duty: they can feed wildlife and also give them cover.

The cover found in your yard will often serve as a safe place for animals to nest or raise their young. You can also build or buy nest boxes and birdhouses. (*See page 27, "Squirrels Need Houses, Too," and page 35, "Birdhouse Basics."*)

Your backyard may qualify as a wildlife habitat with the National Wildlife Federation. Check their web site or contact them about their Backyard Wildlife Habitat Program.

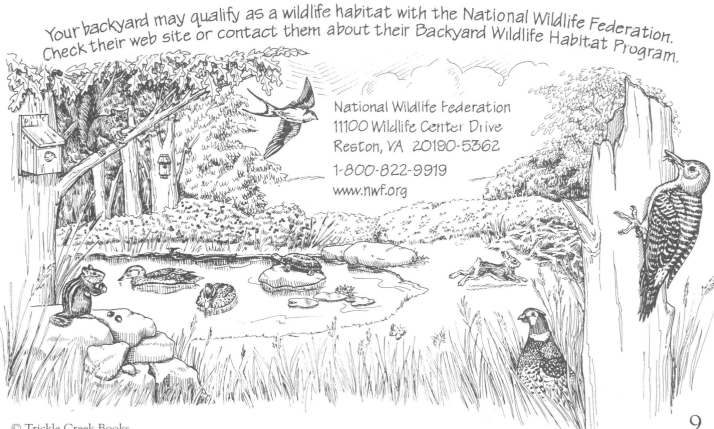

National Wildlife Federation
11100 Wildlife Center Drive
Reston, VA 20190-5362
1-800-822-9919
www.nwf.org

© Trickle Creek Books

# Spring EcoJournal

_____

_____

_____

_____

_____

_____

_____

_____

_____

_____

_____

*March 18:* It was too cold and rainy today to go outside. I was glad to be looking out at the gray, drizzly world from my office upstairs. First I saw a red-bellied woodpecker feeding on the pine outside my window. Its red-capped head was bobbing like a hammer as it chopped at the tree, looking for grubs and insects under the bark. The bird was so close that I could admire the zebra stripes on its back.

About mid-morning, five deer came to eat shelled corn at the deer feeder. At this time of year, their coats are silvery brown and shaggy. Today they were also wet. They looked a little forlorn, but not as miserable as Bailey, my white cat.

When Bailey wants in, he always finds a way to tell me—even when I'm working upstairs. He climbs the maple tree, leaps onto the roof, parades over the peak, drops down a level to the first-floor roof below my office window, and stands up on his hind feet to peer inside. I looked up from my writing to see a soaked cat-face staring at me pitifully. When I opened the window, he streaked in, leaving muddy paw prints on my books and papers.

Not long after Bailey was towel-dried and purring, I had another visitor. A gray squirrel jumped onto the roof from the pine and boldly pressed its face against the window pane. I sat very still while it looked with bright brown eyes into every corner of the room. What a nice day this has turned out to be!

© Trickle Creek Books

# Be a Blind Observer

A blind, or a hide, is a place where you can observe wildlife without being seen. To make a blind, find a hiding place in tall grass or brush. Then cover it with dead branches and debris. From your cozy, secret place, you can observe and photograph the animals that come near.

You can also make a semi-permanent blind by building a small frame and covering it with burlap or an old dark-colored sheet. Throw leaves and brush over the whole hut. Make sure you cut slits or eyeholes at standing and sitting levels. You might want a box or shelf inside the blind to use as a table for your equipment: binoculars, camera, sketchbook, eco-journal, and snacks. A sturdy tree house—checked by an adult for safety—also makes an ideal blind. (When you're in a tree, look for squirrel scratchings.)

Once your blind is built, don't go near it for several days. Let the animals in the area get used to it. Then quietly enter the blind just before dawn or dusk when animals are most active. Wait patiently, listen carefully, and watch. Think of yourself as being invisible or as part of the natural surroundings. You may be amazed at what you see—even in a backyard blind. There are often opossums, raccoons, and skunks living in town.

Good places to set up a blind are near a pond or stream or at the edge of a woods.

To make a Mole Dome, cut a clear plastic soda bottle

to get a piece like this.

Gently dig away a little segment of a mole trail and insert the Mole Dome.

It takes a lot of watching to see a mole go by!

© Trickle Creek Books

# Spring EcoJournal

_____

_____

_____

_____

_____

_____

_____

_____

_____

_____

_____

*March 20:* This is the first day of spring—and my birthday—and our wedding anniversary. It's a special day on the calendar, but the earth is still sleepy, just rubbing its eyes. The landscape looks wintry. There are no wildflowers blooming and the first green on the floor of the woods hasn't yet spread to the next layer, the shrubs.

The only colors, little puddles of colors, are found in the early crocuses. The faithful crocuses, grape-colored, yellow-gold, or white, will bloom beneath the snow and bravely lift their faces to the sun. We enjoy them so much.

I don't plant many tulips any more. It's hardly worth the effort. Two years ago, I planted a hundred tulip bulbs at the bottom of our drive. During the winter, the squirrels ate most of the bulbs and replanted the others, the way they bury nuts for a hungry day. When the tulips bloomed, they looked ridiculous. Instead of a showy bed of bright flowers, I had single tulips scattered through the woods—one at the base of a tree, two beside the creek, one in a little clearing, and so on. When I decided to cut them and at least bring them together in a single container, I found that the deer and rabbits had eaten them all!

Tulips must be tasty. The deer will come right up to the house to dine on tulips, but they leave daffodils and hyacinths alone.

12

© Trickle Creek Books

# Strange Growings

While you're still waiting for spring growth to get going outside, you can do some growing inside. Plant some birdseed in a container of soil. When the weather is warmer, transplant some of the little plants outside in a sunny area. You may be able to grow your own birdseed.

Plant an amaryllus bulb, which you can buy at a garden center. The flower stem grows so fast you can almost see it happening. It may grow one to two inches in a single day! In an amazingly short time, you will have big gorgeous flowers. It's fun to record the plant's growth by making a graph, taking daily photos, or making drawings to scale.

You can grow fresh sprouts to eat in just a few days. Put a tablespoon of alfalfa seeds in a pint jar of water. Let them soak overnight. In the morning, fasten a piece of cheesecloth over the mouth of the jar with a rubber band and pour off the water. Place the jar on its side in a closet or dark place. Twice a day for three days, rinse the sprouts by adding warm water to the jar and then pouring it off. When the seeds have sprouted, put them near a sunny window, so that they will turn green. Then eat them. Sprouts can be sprinkled on any kind of salad, tucked into a sandwich, or used to make Sprout Outs (crackers spread with peanut butter, cream cheese, or cheese spread and topped with sprouts).

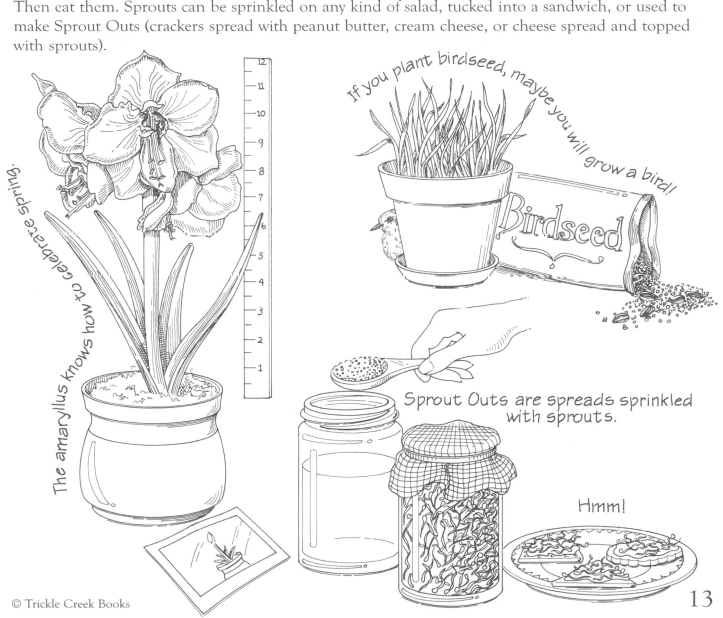

The amaryllus knows how to celebrate spring.

If you plant birdseed, maybe you will grow a bird!

Birdseed

Sprout Outs are spreads sprinkled with sprouts.

Hmm!

© Trickle Creek Books

# Spring EcoJournal

_____

_____

_____

_____

_____

_____

_____

_____

_____

_____

_____

_____

_____

_____

_____

_____

_____

*March 24:* In 1996 on this very date, Bob and I went comet hunting. Comet Hyakutake was supposed to be visible in our night sky as it drew near Earth—well, as near as 9.3 million miles. We dressed warmly, packed our binoculars, and drove to a high, open meadow. (Our view of the sky from Trickle Creek is limited to a few stars peeking through the dark branches of trees.)

We shivered as we searched the sky with our binoculars. A faraway chorus of spring peepers barely broke into the cold silence. I felt so tiny and lonely looking from Earth into the immense space that surrounds us, tinier than a little frog who dares to sing by the light of a comet.

Comet Hyakutake looked like a bright star moving across the sky with a long hazy glow—its tail—following it. It was exciting to see the comet, but my biggest discovery came afterwards when Bob told me to look at the moon through binoculars. I was amazed to see the moon craters and the moon terrain that I had only seen in photos before. Suddenly our vast, daunting universe became a little more knowable.

© Trickle Creek Books

# Early Spring Activities

In early spring when you are starving for color, you can trick the first buds into opening. Cut a few long twigs with buds from a tree or bush. It's fun to choose twigs from a pussy willow, a fruit tree, or a forsythia. Put the twigs in a jar of water and keep them inside where it is warm and light.

Watch for the first tiny leaves to appear on a favorite tree. Then each week, pick one leaf from the tree and draw around it on a large sheet of paper. Don't stop until the leaves are full-size.

See if you can observe a robin catching a worm or insect. If the robin eats the worm immediately, there are probably no young. But if the robin flies away with a worm in the same direction again and again, you know it is feeding baby robins in its nest.

It's like keeping a baby book for a leaf.

Watch the buds open and rejoice!

Watch for the first robin—a sure sign of spring!

© Trickle Creek Books

# Spring EcoJournal

_____

_____

_____

_____

_____

_____

_____

_____

_____

_____

_____

*March 29:* I got up early to make a fifty-mile drive to a school where I was going to give two assemblies. I always like early morning drives, watching the darkness give way to light and seeing the sun rise. The first faint light revealed a world of delicate, icy sparkles. Every tree, every branch, every separate pine needle was lined with ice. The entire world looked like a scene made of the finest glass.

Driving wasn't as dangerous as I expected, and once I was on well cleared highways, I marveled at the landscape. I've only seen this icy condition half a dozen times in my life. The bedraggled dried grasses and wildflowers that stand through the winter were exquisitely dressed in ice. Pinecones and fragile red maple blossoms wore the same sparkling ice-clothing. How beautiful! Isn't it fun to see familiar things in a different way?

To reach the school I was visiting, I had to drive through a mountain pass that goes through a deep woods. Some of the trees that grow along the banks of the road were broken and even uprooted by the weight of the ice on their limbs and branches. The road was an obstacle course with trees lying full-length across it, some from the right and some from the left. First the cars going south worked their way through the course and then the cars going north took a turn— all without any help from the police or a road crew. It was very orderly. By the time I returned home in the afternoon, the pass was clear, the ice had melted, and the sun was shining on the world as it was.

© Trickle Creek Books

# Can't Wait to Plant

There is a time when spring seems to tease us. Tiny green seedlings poke through the earth and tightly packaged buds begin to unfold, but the ground is still cold, and snow and frost are not yet strangers. It won't be time to plant flower or vegetable gardens for more than a month. But if you're impatient to get things growing, there are a few things you can plant right now.

This is a great time to plant a tree. Even if you feel as if you're planting a knobby stick, you can be sure that there are leaves and blossoms and seeds just waiting to happen. To plant the tree, dig a hole big enough to receive the roots without crowding them. Pack about two-thirds of the soil tightly around the roots so there are no air pockets, pour in a bucket of water, and then fill the hole with soil. Sprinkle a handful of fertilizer around the tree and water it into the soil. Finally, build a saucer around the little trunk of the tree to hold rain.

You can also plant early spring vegetables, such as radishes, lettuces, and spinach, especially if you protect them in a cold frame. (A cold frame is usually a shallow box covered with glass, which protects plants and seedlings outdoors.) If you plant a small salad garden, you can use a clear plastic umbrella for a cold frame. Simply take the handle off the umbrella and push the center pole into the ground where you planted your seeds. The umbrella will keep the soil—and later the seedlings—warm and moist. You can lift the umbrella to water the plants occasionally. On an unusually warm day, tip the umbrella to let the heat out. Harvest the greens when they are leafy and tender, and harvest the radishes when the red bulbs begin to show above ground.

A clear plastic umbrella is like a little greenhouse.

Doesn't it feel good to plant a tree?

RED MAPLE

It's fun to carve a radish with a tiny knife or round toothpick.

Salad Dressing

© Trickle Creek Books

# Spring EcoJournal

_____

_____

_____

_____

_____

_____

_____

_____

_____

_____

_____

_____

_____

_____

_____

*April 3:* On my walk today, I saw solid signs of spring. The underbrush has its first tiny leaves, which create a delicate green haze from a distance. And the willow, the first tree to get its leaves and the last to lose them, is golden barked and pushing leaves. In the woods, spring begins on the forest floor and works its way up. That way, the tiny plants on the ground get enough sun to grow and flower before the trees begin to shade them.

I saw a squirrel carrying a great mouthful of dried leaves for a nest. And I saw two mourning doves preening and grooming each other. (There may be a nest in their future, too.) I saw earthworms on the road; their hibernation is over. But the most interesting spring sign—one I have never witnessed before—was something Bob discovered.

I found Bob in the orchard when I returned from walking and the first thing he said was, "I smell a turtle." I've never smelled a turtle, even when I'm holding one in my hands, but when Bob says there is a turtle nearby, there is. His nose is always right. We began to look for the turtle but we couldn't find it. We looked more closely, even moving a mat of leaves aside to look under them. And there it was—a mud-covered, half-buried box turtle, peering up at us with its bright red eyes. Was it just emerging from its winter hibernation?

© Trickle Creek Books

# A Worm Is a Sign of Spring

During winter, earthworms hibernate deep underground. It takes a warm spring day—or a spring rain—to bring them to the surface. Worms on the sidewalk are a sure sign of spring.

The lowly earthworm is the best builder of healthy soil, which nourishes healthy plants. Charles Darwin, a famous naturalist, said that no other animal has played such an important part in world history. If you grow worms in a worm box, you can find out for yourself how worms work the soil, fertilize it with their rich castings, and make spaces for air and water to enter the soil.

To make a worm box, choose a clear plastic container with a lid. Punch drainage holes in the bottom of the container with a hammer and nail. And punch air holes in the lid, too. Fill the container with a layer of gravel, a thin layer of sand, a layer of soil, and a layer of peat moss. Use a spray bottle to moisten the soil with water. On the surface of the soil, spread dead leaves and grass and food scraps (potato peels, apple cores, carrot tops, lettuce leaves—even coffee grounds—but not meat or dairy products). Wait a couple of days before adding the worms.

You can find earthworms in your garden or lawn, or you can buy red worms at a bait shop or nursery. Put six to twelve worms in your worm box. Make sure the soil is moist. Put the lid on the box. Then wrap black fabric or black paper completely around the box to make it dark. Keep the worm box where it is not too hot or too cold, always keep the soil moist, and feed the worms at least once a week.

When you want to observe the worms and their worm-work, remove the black covering. Watch what happens to the different layers of soil and to the food and yard scraps. Look for tunnels, worm castings at the surface, and tiny yellow-green, lemon-shaped cocoons. Two to ten little worms will emerge from a cocoon after about a month of incubation.

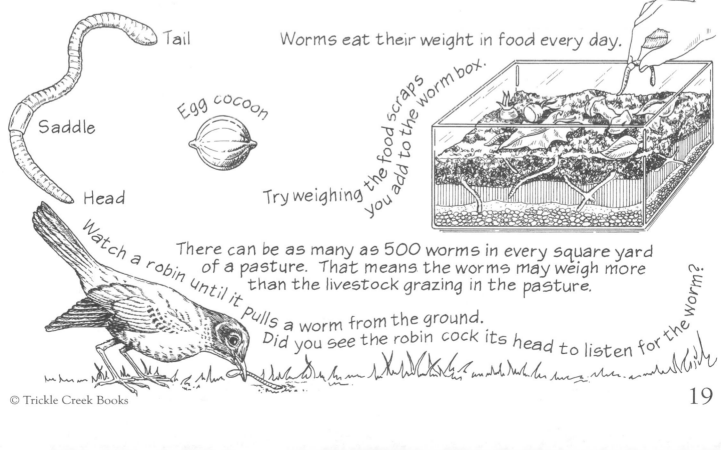

Tail

Saddle

Head

Egg cocoon

Worms eat their weight in food every day.

Try weighing the food scraps you add to the worm box.

Watch a robin until it pulls a worm from the ground.

There can be as many as 500 worms in every square yard of a pasture. That means the worms may weigh more than the livestock grazing in the pasture.

Did you see the robin cock its head to listen for the worm?

© Trickle Creek Books

# Spring EcoJournal

_____

_____

_____

_____

_____

_____

_____

_____

_____

_____

*April 9:* We cleaned out the birdhouses today, and it was cold work. In fact, a light snowfall continued all afternoon. The snow dusted the red maple blossoms, the tiny green flowers on the spice bushes, and the golden, drooping willows. They reminded me of sugarcoated gumdrops, red, green, and yellow.

There was one nest that we didn't disturb today, although last winter, Bob accidentally brought it into the house. One evening when we wanted to use the fireplace, Bob removed some insulation that was stuffed into the fireplace air-intake hole. As he carried it into the basement, he felt something moving inside it. He pulled the insulation open, expecting to see a nest of mice, but two Carolina wrens flew out! They flew in different directions, but one wren called to its mate until they were together again.

We couldn't get the wrens out of the house that night, so they spent the night in the basement with Bailey, the white cat. The night passed without a problem and in the morning, with the basement doors and windows open, one wren flew out and called to the other until it found the way, too.

Bob returned the insulation to its original position, and the wrens continued to sleep there at night for the rest of the winter. Sometimes we would go out after dark with a flashlight, gently open the soft stuffing, and see the Carolina wrens snuggled together inside. Weren't they smart to find such a warm winter hideaway?

20

© Trickle Creek Books

# Ready for Nests

In early spring, the birdhouses that were used last year must be given a spring cleaning for this year's tenants. Wear gloves for this job. You may have to evict a family of mice, but don't worry, they'll find a new home. Pull all of the old nesting materials from the birdhouse. Then use a hose to spray the house inside and out until every corner is clean.

Another way to invite birds to nest in your yard is to provide nest-building materials that will interest them. You can put out bits of string and yarn, strips of cloth, hair, lint from the clothes dryer, dried grass or straw, and pieces of moss. Hang the materials near your birdfeeder in a mesh bag or a basket or draped over a pinecone suspended on a string.

Don't quit feeding the birds. There may still be late snows. And when nesting birds have a ready supply of food, they don't have to spend as much time away from their eggs. Then there is a better chance of hatching all of the eggs successfully.

Robins choose some of the worst places to build nests.

No one wants to move into a messy house.

It's fun to see which birds take which materials.

© Trickle Creek Books

# Spring EcoJournal

_____

_____

_____

_____

_____

_____

_____

_____

_____

_____

_____

_____

_____

_____

*April 13:* We drove to Laurel Lake, which is about an hour away, and had a wonderful morning hike and spring picnic. I was delighted to find the first early wildflowers: tiny spring-beauties, yellow trout-lilies, and bright fat dandelions.

As we crossed a little creek, we met a group of young children playing along the bank. I asked them, "See any tadpoles?" They just stared at me in astonishment. We stood looking at each other for a moment. I couldn't think why they were so surprised at such a simple question. Then the oldest child, who was about five, said, "Come see," and led me down to the water. As we approached, I thought I saw a dark, rippling shadow on the water. Then I thought it was a black plastic garbage bag floating on the surface. And finally I saw thousands—possibly millions—of black tadpoles pushing and wiggling and swimming together. No wonder the children were speechless when I asked if they had seen any tadpoles.

After we returned home, I kept remembering that remarkable tadpole soup and I wondered what was going on in our own pond. Even though it was dark, I was so curious that I decided to walk down to the pond with a flashlight. I took Abercrombie with me. He liked the idea of a night walk and I could hear him crashing through the underbrush on his side trips. I couldn't see tadpoles in the pond, but the night was shrill with the voices of spring peepers. I stood still, listening and smiling in the dark. The night was cold and perfectly clear, and the little frogs and the stars sang together.

© Trickle Creek Books

# Try a Tadpole

As long as there have been kids and tadpoles, kids have been fascinated by tadpoles. And perhaps tadpoles have been fascinated by kids! We don't know.

If you have never watched a slippery little head-with-a-tail change into a fat-bellied frog, it is time for you to try it. The first step is to visit a pond in early spring to collect frog or toad eggs, or *spawn*. Frog spawn looks like a mass of cloudy jelly; toad spawn looks like long strings of black beads; and newt spawn is found as single eggs, each surrounded by clear jelly. Collect about a handful of one kind of spawn. (Don't mix frog and toad or newt spawn in the same container.) Put the spawn in a gallon jar or aquarium filled with pond water, and add some water weed.

Your part in growing little frogs is easy. Keep the aquarium out of direct sunlight. Change the water once a week—always using pond water, not tap water. And once the tadpoles have hatched, provide water plants or decaying lettuce for them to eat. When the tadpoles begin to grow their back legs, their diet will change to meat. You can hang a small piece of meat in the water. Or simply feed them bits of dog or cat food.

As the tadpoles lose their tails and begin to breathe air, place rocks in the aquarium so that they can climb out of the water. Keep the aquarium covered or they may jump out. When the young frogs become this active, it is time to release them at the pond where you collected the spawn. Then they will be in the right environment to catch the insects they need to eat. Releasing tiny frogs in this way—after keeping them safe from predators while they were growing—is helpful to the frog population, which sadly is declining.

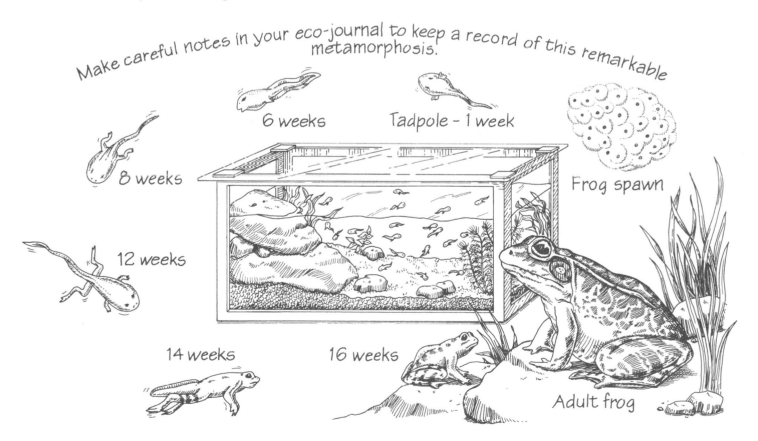

Make careful notes in your eco-journal to keep a record of this remarkable metamorphosis.

6 weeks

Tadpole - 1 week

8 weeks

Frog spawn

12 weeks

14 weeks

16 weeks

Adult frog

© Trickle Creek Books

# Spring EcoJournal

_____

_____

_____

_____

_____

_____

_____

_____

_____

_____

_____

*April 15:* I had a special reason for walking to the pond this morning. I wanted to see a spring peeper. The peeper chorus fills the air with frog music. Surely there are hundreds, even thousands, of little frogs shouting their songs, but where are they when I look for them? They are so difficult to spot.

As I approached the pond, the singing died down to silence. The peepers were hiding. I sat still on the cold ground until they forgot me and started calling again. I was running my eyes over the shrubs and grasses, looking for one of the tiny tree frogs, when a drop of water caught my attention. It was a raindrop hanging off the end of a leaf. And reflected in it, I could see the pond, the trees around it, and the sky above it—only they were all upside down. How interesting!

It reminded me of another discovery that a group of children made. (I've always found that children are excellent observers. They see everything.) We were looking for mushrooms when a little girl pointed to what looked like tiny bird's nests filled with eggs. They were so small that ten of the little "nests" would fit on a nickel. We looked them up in a field guide to mushrooms and what do you think? They were called bird's nest fungi. The "eggs" were little packets of spores, the microscopic seeds of the mushrooms.

Undistracted by water drops and memories of mushrooms, I finally saw a little peeper hanging on a blade of grass. It was about an inch long with a dark X on its back. I found you.

© Trickle Creek Books

# Tiny Treasures

It's only "natural" to enjoy nature, but to really be a skilled nature watcher, you need to sharpen all your senses and learn to be alert and observant. Of course it's wonderful to have a teacher to help you—a trained nature guide or a friend who knows about animals and plants in your area. But you can also train yourself. Try some of the exercises below.

Go on a tiny treasure hunt. Take a bag to hold what you collect, but not just any bag. Use one of the tiny paper or plastic bags that holds a spare button and is attached to a new shirt or sweater. These little bags are usually about 1½ inches by 2½ inches. Look for treasures that will fit into the bag, such as the littlest mushroom or berry or stone.

In spring, a good way to teach yourself to spot something unusual and small, too, is to look for eggshells from bird eggs. After baby birds hatch, the parent birds often take the eggshells out of the nest and drop them in another location to keep predators from finding the nest. Keep your eyes open for eggshells wherever you walk.

After it rains, examine drops of water that have collected on leaves and flowers and grasses. Look for a reflection in the water drop. Can you see yourself? Raise your hand and watch the tiny movement reflected in the drop. Can you see scenery? Is it right side up or upside down?

Sit outside and close your eyes but open your ears. Listen carefully to the sounds around you and try to identify each one. At other times when you are hiking or playing outside, remind yourself to really listen to the wind, to rain, and to water. Smell them too. Don't you love the smell of fresh-cut grass or rain on a dusty road or the salty smell of the ocean! Train yourself to use all your senses, including your senses of wonder and curiosity, and you'll be a great nature watcher.

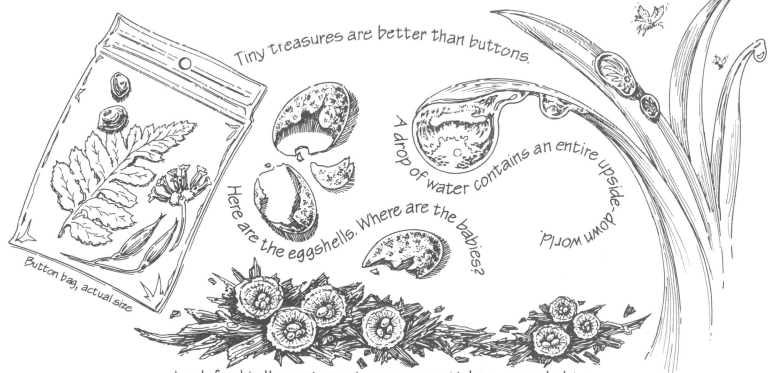

Tiny treasures are better than buttons.

Button bag, actual size

Here are the eggshells. Where are the babies?

A drop of water contains an entire upside-down world.

Look for bird's nest mushrooms on sticks or wood chips.

© Trickle Creek Books

# Spring EcoJournal

_____

_____

_____

_____

_____

_____

_____

_____

_____

*April 17:* This is the day when the baby squirrels are finally peeking out of the entrance hole of their squirrel house. I've been waiting and waiting! First there was one little face, then two. Then three faces crowded and pressed together, competing for a first look at the leafy world around them. They're as cute as baby bunnies—with shortened faces and big brown eyes. I watched them all morning from my office window and remembered....

Several years ago, we saw a young squirrel fall twenty feet to the ground. When we rushed outside, we found the little animal bright-eyed but unable to move. We contacted the Humane Society, who sent "the squirrel lady," an expert at rehabilitating injured squirrels. She found that the squirrel couldn't move its back legs or tail but that it could use its front legs. She was pleased at how well we were caring for the squirrel, so after giving us detailed advice, she left it in our care.

We called the little squirrel Feisty because it was so lively, spunky, and bold. I kept her in my office in a fiberglass travel kennel, so that she couldn't chew her way out. At first, it was only furnished with wood chips and a soft baby blanket. But gradually Feisty collected other things for her home. She usually explored my office while I worked, and one day she found a rawhide bone that the dog had left on the floor. She worked hard to drag the bone, which was as long as she was, into her kennel. She loved to chew on it—although Abercrombie was not happy to find his bone in her cage. With his nose against the door of the kennel, he spent hours watching her chew.

© Trickle Creek Books

# Squirrels Need Houses, Too

If you live where there are big hardwood trees, especially oaks, ash, elms, and gum trees, you probably see squirrels in your neighborhood. They may live in hollows in the sides of the hardwood trees or, as a second choice, they might build leaf nests in the tops of tall trees. Their leaf nests are snug and warm, but they can be damaged or ruined by high winds. A leaf nest is not an ideal place to raise a litter of baby squirrels.

It's great fun to provide a nest box for squirrels, because it will give you an opportunity to observe them closely. First the squirrels will cautiously investigate the house you build for them. When they decide to move in, you can watch them carry enormous bundles of leaves in their mouths to furnish their home. Eventually, a litter of babies will appear and the first tiny faces with big brown eyes will peek out the entrance hole to see what the world has to offer. Day by day, the little squirrels will explore more, first climbing onto the roof of their house and then onto the tree it is fastened to and finally playing recklessly on every limb.

A squirrel house should be made of 1-inch lumber, not sanded smooth. The entrance hole should be 3 inches in diameter and facing south. (*See page 55 for nest box requirements for a Gray Squirrel.*) The house should be placed 20 to 30 feet above ground on a tree at least 10 inches in diameter and close to a branch, so the squirrels can easily dart inside. Gray Squirrels like to have their homes 50 yards or more inside a wooded area. Fox Squirrels like to live at the edge of a woods.

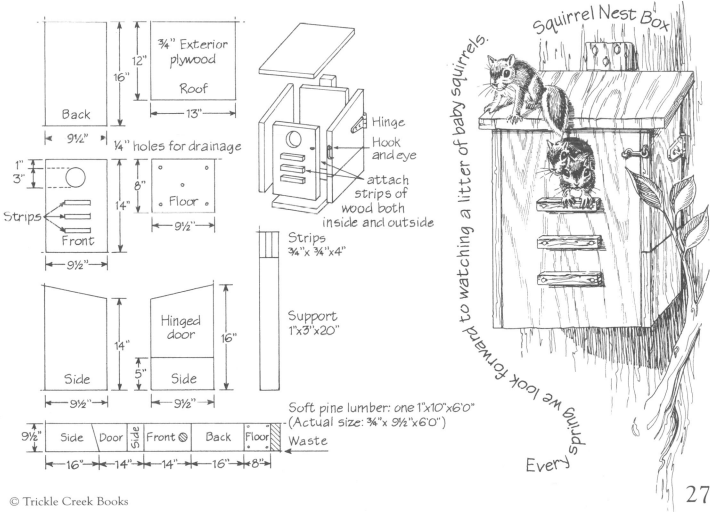

© Trickle Creek Books

# Spring EcoJournal

_____

_____

_____

_____

_____

_____

_____

_____

_____

_____

_____

_____

_____

_____

*April 18 (Feisty's story continued):* One day as I worked at the computer, Feisty gripped my sweatshirt with her front feet and climbed up my back. As she balanced on my shoulder, I held my breath. I was thinking about how powerful a squirrel's teeth are—strong enough to open a black walnut. But then I had a wonderful thought: "There is a baby squirrel sitting on my shoulder!" And I loved it. In the days and weeks that followed, I got used to her climbing up my back and watching me work.

Once we knew she could climb, we brought a sturdy branch with rough bark into the office. We leaned the six-foot branch in a corner and fluffed a soft blanket around the base. Feisty was a good climber, but without the use of her tail for balance, she often ended up bouncing into the blanket. She also fell from my desk into the wastebasket at least once a day. I wondered if she did it on purpose. She liked playing with the waste paper until the wastebasket would turn over and she could escape.

We tried to "listen" to her behavior, so that we would know how best to care for her. She told us that she needed to chew (remember the rawhide bone she stole?) and that she needed to climb. She told us that she liked to be petted but not held. And she told us exactly what she liked to eat. Her favorite treat was sunflower seeds, but she also ate nuts, cereal, dried corn, and fruit. We hid some of her food, so that she could gather it and store it the way all squirrels do.

© Trickle Creek Books

# Wise Care for Wounded Wildlife

It is distressing to find a wounded animal. We want to try to help—but how? What is the best and wisest thing to do?

A bird or mammal that is so hurt that it can't fly or run away is seriously injured or sick. Get help from an adult to gently lift the animal into a box lined with a soft towel. Since a helpless animal is naturally frightened and defensive, the adult should wear heavy work gloves to avoid getting bitten. Place the box in a warm, quiet place away from people.

You may want to feed and nurse the animal you rescue, but it takes special knowledge and skill to save a wild animal. Call the Humane Society, SPCA, Audubon Society, or a veterinarian for help. They will be able to put you in contact with a *rehabilitator*, a person who is experienced in caring for the kind of animal you found. Rehabilitators also have state permits to keep wildlife in captivity. *Note:* Once the rescued animal is settled with the rehabilitator, you can take the opportunity to ask some questions. Find out how the animals are cared for and where they are released. Maybe the rehabilitator will tell you some stories about other rescued animals. Maybe he or she will invite you to call and check on the progress of the animal you found.

Sometimes a bird, seeing a reflection of itself or the sky or trees in a window, will crash into the window and fall to the ground. If the bird is alive but unconscious, you will need to protect it until it regains consciousness. Get any cats or dogs out of the way. Gently pick the bird up, take it inside where it is warm and quiet, and place it on a sheet of newspaper. Put a colander (or even a light box) over the bird until it begins to cheep or flutter its wings. Then you will have the joy of releasing it!

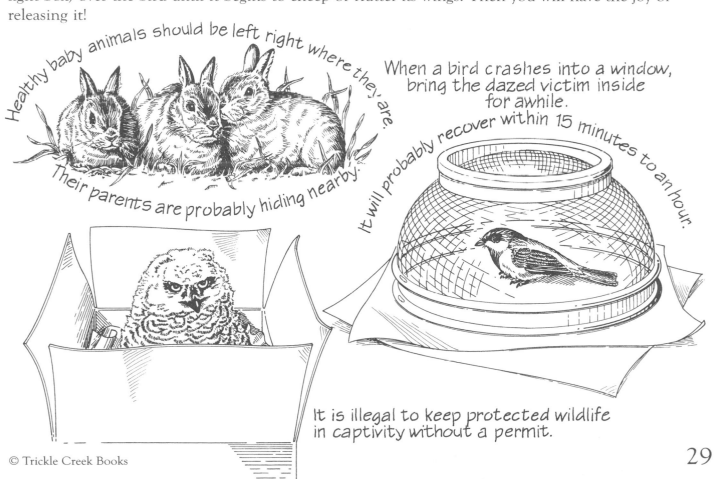

Healthy baby animals should be left right where they are. Their parents are probably hiding nearby.

When a bird crashes into a window, bring the dazed victim inside for awhile. It will probably recover within 15 minutes to an hour.

It is illegal to keep protected wildlife in captivity without a permit.

© Trickle Creek Books

# Spring EcoJournal

_____

_____

_____

_____

_____

_____

_____

_____

_____

*April 19 (**Feisty's story concluded**):* One day when I heard Feisty scolding the dog with a husky barking call, I recognized the sound that an adult squirrel makes. Feisty was still small, although her shoulders and front legs were sturdy and strong. I hadn't realized until I heard her grown-up voice that she was grown.

Bob built a large cage for Feisty, so that we could introduce her to the outdoors. We placed a squirrel house (like the one in which she was born) inside the cage, as well as tree branches, water and food, and the baby blanket from her kennel. We even supplied a box of dirt so she could bury nuts. She spent several days moving into the squirrel house. She stripped leaves from the branches and made a nest with them. And she pulled the blanket inside, too!

An interesting thing happened when Feisty moved outside. She had a daily visitor. An adult squirrel spent time with her every morning. I wondered if the squirrel might be her mother. Young squirrels stay with their mother for a season, and sometimes we see them playing together.

We tried to make Feisty's life in captivity as interesting as possible. We gave her unusual foods to try and natural objects to investigate. We occasionally brought her into the house, but she wasn't really comfortable there any longer. One evening, I tried to call her out of her squirrel house, but she didn't appear. The next morning I found her dead. We wrapped her in the baby blanket and laid her in a little grave lined with ferns. And we said good-bye to a dear friend.

Wild Geranium

Columbine

Jack-in-the-Pulpit

Virginia Bluebell

Spring Beauty

Painted Trillium

Fern Fiddlehead

Violet

© Trickle Creek Books

# Save the Whales and the Wildflowers

If you were asked to name an endangered species, would you think of a wildflower? We need to remember that more and more wildflowers and wild plants, as well as animals, are harmed by polluted air, acid rain, pesticides and herbicides in runoff, and loss of habitat. You can find out which wildflowers in your state are becoming rare or endangered by calling your state environmental agency or your local Sierra Club or Audubon Society.

When you pick wildflowers, think carefully about what you are doing. Never take wildflowers from a state or national park, where they are protected by law. Don't disturb wildflowers that are officially listed as becoming rare, or flowers that are growing sparsely (only one or two plants blooming in a large area). Don't pull wildflowers up by the roots or take all the flowers on a single plant.

This doesn't mean that we can't ever gather wildflowers. There is a special delight in taking home a dazzling bouquet that we didn't buy or grow, one that reminds us of the fragile beauty and wild exuberance of nature. And we can always collect *rare* wildflowers by taking photographs or making detailed sketches of them.

When you take a photo or make a sketch of a wildflower, record the name of the flower, the date, and where you found it.

April 27
Dutchman's Breeches
Shenk's Ferry
Wildflower Preserve

May 2
Wild Blue Phlox
Pinchot Park

Color Queen Anne's Lace by putting the stems in water dyed with food coloring. In just a few hours, the flowers will be tinted.

Make a tiny bouquet of woods flowers and give it to a special friend.

Feisty

© Trickle Creek Books

# Spring EcoJournal

_____

_____

_____

_____

_____

_____

_____

_____

*April 22:* Margaret and I spent all day at Shenk's Ferry Wildflower Preserve. (Margaret is the illustrator of this book.) We drove south along the Susquehanna River on winding, hilly country roads. All of the trees are in leaf, the dogwood blossoms are turning white, and the plum trees are in full bloom. There are butter-yellow fields of wild mustard and that unreal green of new spring grass. We drove into a deep woods on a narrow dirt road and found the wildflower preserve at the end.

Spring wildflowers in Pennsylvania are usually small and modest, but for some reason, at Shenk's Ferry the wildflowers all bloom together in a wild array of color and fragrance. Shenk's Ferry is like a tiny hidden valley with steep sides lifting up on either side of a rushing creek. Visitors walk on a path beside the creek with violets, spring-beauties, and wild geranium at their feet and painted trillium, bright red wild columbine, and funny-looking Dutchman's breeches covering the steep forest floor beside them.

Margaret took photos of the Virginia bluebell with its bright pink buds and of stonecrop sedum nestled in a bed of ferns and soft moss. I made scribbly notes about our day. I wrote: All of our senses are satisfied. We hear the creek laughing. We smell the sweet wet fragrance of morning mist on flowers. A whispering breeze cools our faces. We look and look at the wildflowers. We see purple violets, tiny yellow violets, creamy white violets, and blue and gray Confederate violets. We lift the leaves of the mayapple to see if the flowers or fruit are there. (Not yet!) We look under the hood of the Jack-in-the-pulpit to see if Jack is preaching. (He is!) We touch the cushiony moss to see if it feels like a pillow. (It does!)

© Trickle Creek Books

# Pressed Memories

One way to keep wildflowers for a long time is to press them. Spring wildflowers, which are often small and delicate, are perfect for pressing. Then you can remember them in another season.

The best time to gather wildflowers is at midday when they are dry. Use scissors to cleanly cut everything you want to press—not only flowers, but buds, stems, leaves, tendrils, grasses, ferns, and seedheads. Place them in a rigid plastic container and quickly take them home.

To press flowers between books, you need two big heavy books, newspaper, and tissues. Place a one-inch stack of newspaper on top of one of the books, and lay one tissue on top of the newspaper. Carefully arrange your flowers, plants, and plant parts facedown on the tissue. Cover them with another tissue and another layer of newspaper. Keep making layers of tissues, plants, more tissues, and newspaper until you have used up all your plants. Then put the second book on top of all the layers. Keep the books and flowers in a warm dry place for two to six weeks. You can check them after two weeks. (*You can also press flowers in a flower press. See page 54 for directions on how to build one.*)

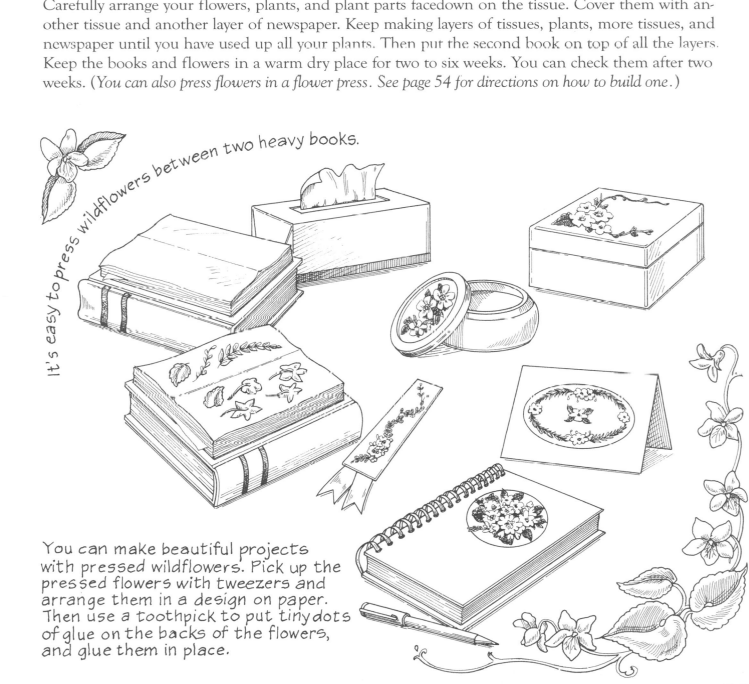

It's easy to press wildflowers between two heavy books.

You can make beautiful projects with pressed wildflowers. Pick up the pressed flowers with tweezers and arrange them in a design on paper. Then use a toothpick to put tiny dots of glue on the backs of the flowers, and glue them in place.

© Trickle Creek Books

# Spring EcoJournal

_____

_____

_____

_____

_____

_____

_____

_____

_____

_____

*April 24:* I didn't get much work done in my office this morning. The little squirrels distracted me. They've been very cautious about coming out of their squirrel house. They *have* to be cautious twenty feet above the ground! Each day, they come farther out of the entrance hole. And finally today they were completely out. Four little squirrels were rushing, pushing, playing, hanging upside down, climbing on their roof, diving back into the entrance hole, and peeking out again. So far, all of their activity has been on the squirrel house. They haven't ventured onto the tree itself.

In the afternoon, Bob and I walked down to the pond. Last fall, we put a large nest box on a tree near the water to attract an interesting animal or bird—a squirrel or raccoon, a pileated woodpecker (the showy "Woody Woodpecker"), a flicker, or a duck. Bob has seen a wood duck on the pond several times and we hoped it might be interested in the nest box. We climbed up to look in the entrance hole. I tapped on the house first, so that we didn't surprise a bird inside. With the help of a mirror, we quietly looked in the nest box and counted ten good-sized eggs, almost the size of small chicken eggs. The cream-colored eggs were laid in a nest of grasses and small downy feathers.

At home, we read about wood ducks. The eggs are the right color, size, and number to belong to a wood duck. We hope they do. The wood duck has been described as "America's most beautiful waterfowl." The male wood duck is the most highly colored duck in North America, and in spring, its colors are indescribable. Wouldn't it be fun to have ten little wood ducks on the pond?

34

© Trickle Creek Books

# Birdhouse Basics

Did you know that every species of bird has its own special requirements for an ideal home? For example, when you build a birdhouse, it's important to use precise measurements for the size of the entrance hole. A wren is comfortable and safe in a house with a 1-inch entrance hole, but a bluebird prefers a 1½-inch hole, and a robin nests in a box with no hole at all. (*Before you build a birdhouse, see page 55 for the nest box requirements for some common birds.*)

Here are some birdhouse basics: (a) Cut out the six parts of the birdhouse. (b) Drill the entrance hole in the front, five ¼-inch holes in the floor for drainage, and several holes near the top of the sides to let fresh air in. (c) Slant the top of each side panel, so that the roof will shed water. The roof should overhang the front about 2 inches. (d) Join the parts together with 2-inch nails placed about 2 inches apart. (e) Hinge one edge of the roof, so that you can easily check or clean the house. Use a hook and eye to keep the roof secure. (f) Don't use stains or wood finishes that contain pentachlorophenol, green preservative, or creosote. (g) Use aluminum nails if you attach the house to a living tree.

Another way to attract birds is to have a messy yard. Birds like to nest and raise their young where they feel safe and sheltered. They look for dense shrubbery, tall trees, brush piles, trunks of dead trees, and high grass. Is there room in your yard for some wilderness?

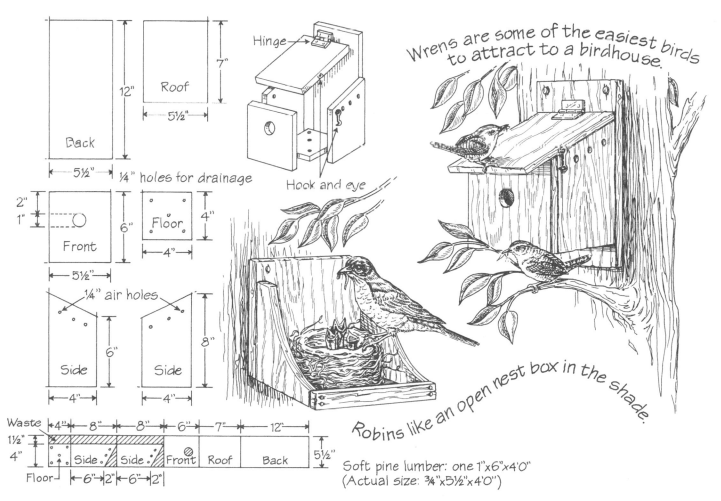

Wrens are some of the easiest birds to attract to a birdhouse.

Robins like an open nest box in the shade.

Soft pine lumber: one 1"x6"x4'0"
(Actual size: ¾"x5½"x4'0")

# Spring EcoJournal

_____

_____

_____

_____

_____

_____

_____

_____

_____

_____

*May 5:* What a beautiful day! The grass is so green you can hardly look at it, the lilacs smell wonderful, and the mayapples are blooming in the woods. Their leaves are like green umbrellas that hide the flowers, but when I lift the leaves, I can see a large white flower shyly nodding underneath.

Bob and I took a "birdhouse tour" today to see who has moved in. A pair of wrens are still building their nest in the birdhouse outside our kitchen window. There was some question about whether the house would be occupied by the wrens or a pair of chickadees. The wrens won the argument and are working industriously.

There are bluebirds in the bluebird house. The male always catches our eye with its beautiful blue cloak worn over a rusty red shirt. We watched the bluebird work hard to build a nest. We laughed when it indignantly chased a squirrel away from its house. And Bob saw it feed its mate long worms. Today we saw the first bluebird egg in the nest. The egg was smaller than a grape—and blue, of course. I'm so glad we built houses for bluebirds. Their natural nesting sites, which are holes in trees, are scarce.

A phoebe, which is a small gray flycatcher, is nesting under the rafters inside the shed. Her nest is neatly made of dried grasses and leaves and soft moss. There are three tiny white eggs in the nest. I hope the eggs and the little birds-to-come will be safe. We've seen a blacksnake sleeping in the rafters. And our cat Bailey loves to sleep up there, too.

© Trickle Creek Books

# No Better Builders

Bird nests are interesting to observe, but it is against the law to collect them. The Migratory Bird Treaty Act is a federal law that makes it illegal to kill, injure, or take any migratory bird or any of its parts (including feathers), its nest, or its eggs. You can see how this law protects the birds we love.

When you come across a bird's nest, don't touch it, but do look at it as closely as you can. Where is it? On the ground, in a shrub, in a tree, at the top of a tree, in a cavity in the tree, in a hole in a dirt bank, on the side of a building? What is it made of? Grass, twigs, leaves, moss, lichen, hair, mud? Is there anything man-made in the nest? Is the inside of the nest lined with something soft, such as downy feathers, animal hair, or spider web?

After you have observed a bird's nest, try to build a nest yourself. First you must find all of the materials. Then you must try to construct a nest that would be strong enough to hold several hungry, elbowing baby birds. Test your handiwork by placing the nest in a tree or shrub and putting one or two chicken eggs from your kitchen in it. Did your nest pass the test?

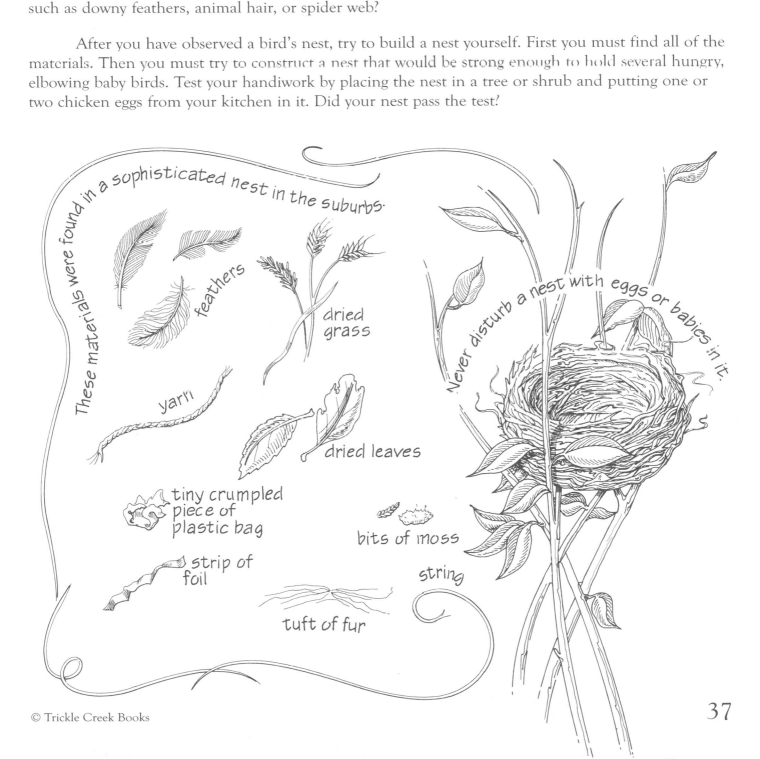

These materials were found in a sophisticated nest in the suburbs.

feathers

dried grass

yarn

dried leaves

tiny crumpled piece of plastic bag

bits of moss

strip of foil

string

tuft of fur

Never disturb a nest with eggs or babies in it.

© Trickle Creek Books

# Spring EcoJournal

_____

_____

_____

_____

_____

_____

_____

_____

_____

_____

_____

**May 11:** In Pennsylvania, spring comes gently, bringing tiny changes day by day for six or seven weeks. It occurs like a sunrise, beginning with the faint gray dawn and bringing more and more warmth and color until the sky is filled with spectacular colored light. By mid-May, spring is glorious!

Shiny buttercups are blooming in emerald-green grass. The showy dame's rockets, looking like long-stemmed phlox, are white, pink, and purple. The dogwood trees have such bright white flowers that we can see them glowing in the dark. Tiny blossoms on the autumn olive fill the air with fragrance.

Today I planted my garden. It's a small garden right in the middle of the lawn. With so many tall trees around us, that's the only place that gets any sun. I worked for several hours, and as the day wore on, I had company. There were little yellow butterflies and two cottontail rabbits playing on the lawn. The baby squirrels are exploring their tree. I saw white-tailed deer browsing at the edge of the lawn. They look shaggy and scruffy, because they haven't got their summer coats yet. In the distance, I saw a fat young groundhog rolling along in the orchard like a brown bowling ball.

Two years ago, I planted a kitchen garden with lettuce, tomatoes, green onions, and carrots. Last year, I planted a wildflower garden. This year, I planted bright annual flowers with a wild mixture of colors. Actually, all of my gardens are the same. They are "Animal Food Gardens."  The deer, the rabbits, the squirrels, and the groundhogs—not to mention the opossums, raccoons, and skunks—think that whatever I plant in my garden is tastier than _anything_ in the woods.

© Trickle Creek Books

# More Gardens Than Stars

If you plant a garden, make it your own. Make it a little different from any other garden in the world. There is no limit to what you can do. You can plant vegetables to make a Salad Garden, a Soup Garden, an Ethnic Garden, or a This-Is-the-Only-Vegetable-I-Like Garden. You could even make an elaborate Knot Garden with herbs.

You can choose silvery plants and grasses and white flowers for a Moonlight Garden to be viewed in the moonlight. Or plant flowers that attract butterflies for a Butterfly Garden. Use plants that grow wild in your area to make a Native Garden—a Woodland Border, a Cactus Garden, a Bog Garden, a Meadow Garden, etc. To plant a Wildflower Garden, choose seeds that are packaged for your region. Then your wildflowers will have just the right conditions to grow well, and you will help preserve your native wildflowers.

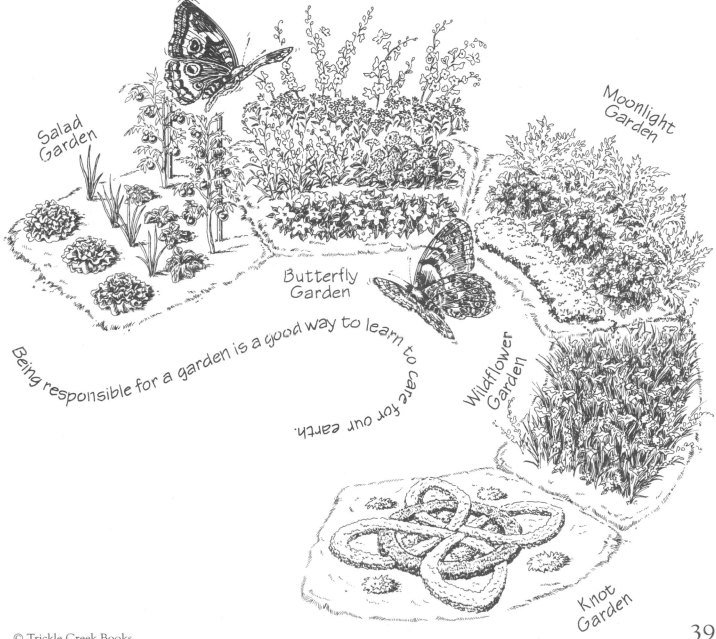

Salad Garden

Moonlight Garden

Butterfly Garden

Being responsible for a garden is a good way to learn to care for our earth.

Wildflower Garden

Knot Garden

© Trickle Creek Books

# Spring EcoJournal

_____

_____

_____

_____

_____

_____

_____

_____

_____

_____

_____

_____

**May 19:** This was the most remarkable day. For one thing, the temperature was in the nineties. Five days ago, we had a late freeze, and we'll probably have more cool weather this month. But today held the promise of summer.

I took a long (warm) walk. I saw a pileated woodpecker—a rare treat. We see oval-shaped holes in the trees made by a pileated woodpecker, but we don't often get our eyes on the bird itself. This woodpecker was as big as a crow, about a foot and a half in length. It had a tall, red crest—_you_ know, a Woody Woodpecker crest. For five minutes, I watched the bird pounding on a fallen log as it searched for insects and grubs. Then the woodpecker gave an eerie and delightful call— like a sound in a rainforest—and flew away.

As I walked through the woods, I noticed that the leaves on the trees are big enough now to give shade. The locust trees are blooming with heavy white blossoms hanging like bunches of white grapes. I stopped to look up into the trees, and when I looked down at the trail again, there was a baby rabbit about five inches long sitting almost at my feet. I knelt down on the path and said out loud, "Well, where did you come from?" I expected the little rabbit to run away, but it didn't. I reached out, gently picked it up, and cradled it against me.

At first I was afraid that the rabbit must be injured, but it looked and felt perfectly healthy. In fact, it had a fat little belly, beautiful soft fur, and bright, curious eyes. When I released it, it ran away like it should have done in the first place. Oh, how innocent a baby bunny is!

40

© Trickle Creek Books

# You Can Raise a Caterpillar

One of the most interesting nature activities you can do is to care for a caterpillar until it becomes a butterfly or moth. If you buy caterpillars from a biological supply company or a nature store, they will come with a supply of food and a suitable container. Your part is simply to watch wide-eyed as the caterpillars grow, build their cocoons or chrysalids, and emerge as new creatures. You might give yourself two assignments while you are raising the caterpillars: (1) keep a careful record in your eco-journal of the changes that occur, and (2) find out where the butterflies live naturally, so that you can release them in the right area—a meadow, roadside, woods, or other area.

It's even more fun to raise a "wild" caterpillar that you find yourself, but this takes a little effort. First you must observe the caterpillar carefully to find out *exactly* what it eats. (It will not grow without the correct plants to feed on.) You should check an insect field guide, too, to identify the caterpillar and read about what it eats. Then you must provide a daily supply of the right plants for the caterpillar's diet. Also sprinkle a little water on the plants for the caterpillar.

You can keep the caterpillar in a terrarium with a screen lid or in a large jar. Cover the jar with muslin or netting secured with a rubber band. Put some compost or soil in the bottom of the container and provide some tiny branches too. Keep the container outside (perhaps on a porch) where the temperature and light are as natural as possible. Don't move the container after the caterpillar becomes a pupa. *Note:* If you find a cocoon rather than a caterpillar, don't try to remove it from the twig or object it is attached to. Put the twig and the cocoon into your terrarium in the same position in which you found them.

When the butterfly or moth emerges with wet wings, it will need enough room in the container to spread its wings and dry them. It's a good idea to release the butterfly quickly, so that it doesn't injure its wings in the container.

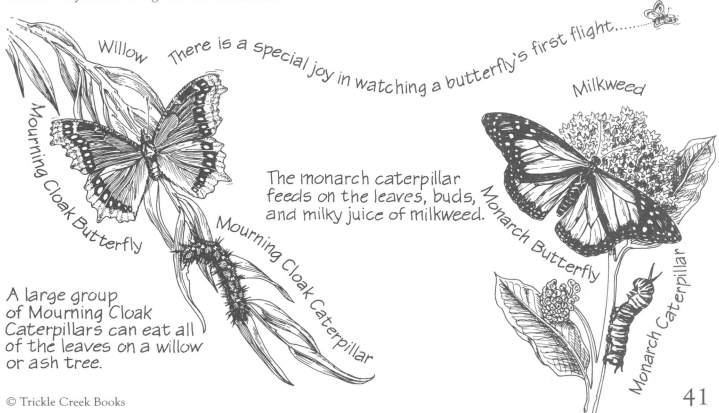

Willow

There is a special joy in watching a butterfly's first flight......

Milkweed

Mourning Cloak Butterfly

Mourning Cloak Caterpillar

The monarch caterpillar feeds on the leaves, buds, and milky juice of milkweed.

Monarch Butterfly

Monarch Caterpillar

A large group of Mourning Cloak Caterpillars can eat all of the leaves on a willow or ash tree.

© Trickle Creek Books

# Spring EcoJournal

_____

_____

_____

_____

_____

_____

_____

_____

_____

_____

_____

**May 20:** Good news and bad news at the pond. First the bad news: Six of the wood duck eggs are gone from the nest box and the other four have been opened and emptied. I wonder if that was the work of a raccoon? I'm so disappointed. I can only hope that the wood ducks will return next year. If we could think of a way to anchor the nest box in the center of the pond, the birds and their young would be safe.

The good news is that I saw a painted turtle sunning itself at the edge of the pond. Two years ago, I bought a painted turtle at a pet store and released it among the cattails in our pond. But until today, I never saw it again. I was thinking about the turtle as I walked through the woods and onto a favorite country road, a dirt road with lots of wildlife. I saw something crossing the road ahead of me. What a surprise to find that it was a painted turtle! I picked it up and carried it back to our pond. Now we have two turtles. (Unless the turtle I found was the turtle I bought—a turtle marathon walker escaping from the pond.)

I have a little "eco-pond" at the bird feeder. It is a plastic dishpan dug into the earth. Since it is under the trees, it is always full of decaying leaves that turn the water a clear, dark brown. Birds, squirrels, and rabbits drink from it daily. And both Abercrombie and Bailey prefer the dark pond water to the fresh water in their bowls. My mother thinks that the decaying leaves add tannic acid to the water. (There is tannic acid in the tea we drink.) Maybe the animals like the eco-pond water because it is a kind of wildlife tea.

© Trickle Creek Books

# Make an Eco-Pond

The smallest, simplest pool of water can be an "eco-pond," which will give you another wild-life ecosystem to observe. Anything that will hold water—a barrel, a plastic kiddie pool, or an old dishpan—can be dug into the ground and made into a little pond. Try not to place your eco-pond under a tree, where it will fill with leaves and debris. If you want to put water lilies or other flowering plants in the pond, place it where it will receive at least six hours of sunlight each day.

If your eco-pond is more than 12 inches deep, it will support both plants and fish. Even a very shallow pond can support bog plants, frogs, and insects. To stock your eco-pond and help it come alive, it's fun to collect water plants, frog eggs, insect larvae, snails, aquatic turtles, crayfish, and minnows from a nearby creek or pond. Feed them packaged fish food once a day until the natural food chain is established. Plant grasses and wildflowers around the edge of the pond and add a rotting log to make the area attractive to amphibians.

Of course you must keep your eco-pond filled with clean water when there is not enough rain to do it for you. If your tap water is chlorinated, let it stand in a container for 24 hours before you add it to the pond. Besides being a miniature water habitat, your eco-pond will provide drinking water for birds and other animals. (Watch for them!)

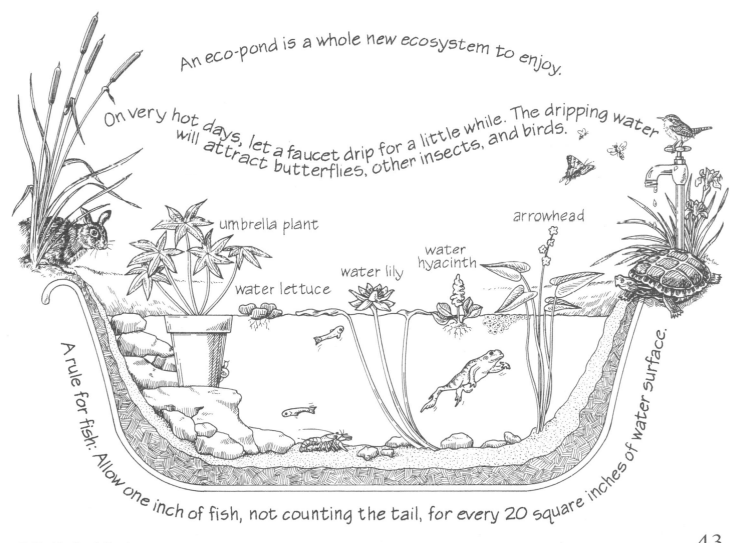

An eco-pond is a whole new ecosystem to enjoy.

On very hot days, let a faucet drip for a little while. The dripping water will attract butterflies, other insects, and birds.

umbrella plant

arrowhead

water hyacinth

water lily

water lettuce

A rule for fish: Allow one inch of fish, not counting the tail, for every 20 square inches of water surface.

© Trickle Creek Books

# Spring EcoJournal

_____

_____

_____

_____

_____

_____

_____

_____

_____

*May 23:* In spring, each day begins with an early morning chorus that swells voice by voice into a great commotion of birdsong. I've never minded waking up to this "joyful noise." But I have to admit that this year I dread the first voice and what follows.

Every morning just before dawn, we hear the voice of a male cardinal, triumphant and challenging, and then a loud "plud" as it hits the glass door of our bedroom with its shoulder and head. For the next ten minutes, it flies into the window, plud, plud, plud, plud, plud. By the time the other birds start singing, we are fully awake and would like to get our hands on that banging red head. The cardinal is a brave red warrior who is determined to keep all other male cardinals out of its territory—especially the one that appears in our window in the first morning light, the one that looks exactly like him, the one that meets him head-on as he attacks. As the day proceeds and the light changes, the cardinal sees its enemy in other windows and attacks again. Plud, plud at the kitchen window, plud, plud, plud, plud at my office window.

We've tried everything we can think of to discourage this miserable warrior. I taped owl silhouettes cut from black paper to some of the windows, but the cardinal is too frantic—or too dazed by all its "pludding"—to be cautious. We've tried closing the blinds, but apparently the bird still sees its reflection. We've hung strips of foil and plastic streamers outside the windows. Our house is decorated like a circus—or a used car lot. And we still live with plud, plud, plud, plud. Our only hope is that after the nesting season, the red warrior will retire.

© Trickle Creek Books

# A Spring Song

Wake up early some spring morning—before dawn—and listen to the first haunting birdsong that breaks the night's silence. Listen as other voices join in, and listen to the full rousing chorus. Try to spot a bird that is singing. This is the best way to learn to identify birdcalls. If you can actually see a bird at the same time you hear it, you will never forget its call.

As you listen to a birdsong, open your mouth (if no one is watching!) and imagine the sound is coming from your own throat. Try to imitate the birdcall by whistling or singing. You may want to buy an Audubon Bird Call from the National Audubon Society. It is a little device that enables you to call small birds to you. Or you could buy a wild turkey call, a duck or goose call, or an owl call at a sporting goods store. You might be able to call in a wild turkey from a field or get a great horned owl to answer you in the woods. An owl call will sometimes attract a number of small protesting song birds, too.

Another way to call birds is to kiss the back of your hand with a small smacking sound or to say, "Pssh, pssh, pssh, pssh" in sets of four. Birds are as curious as cats, and they are often attracted by an interesting sound. Stand quietly near shrubs or trees when you call birds, and see if they will come to you.

A towhee urges, "Drink your TEA."

A white-breasted nuthatch wonders, "To-what, what, what, what, what."

The barred owl worries, "Who cooks for-you? Who cooks for-you-all!?"

"Tea-kettle."

The Carolina wren reminds herself, "Tea-kettle, tea-kettle, tea-kettle."

© Trickle Creek Books

# Spring EcoJournal

_____

_____

_____

_____

_____

_____

_____

_____

_____

_____

**May 25:** I walked on my favorite dirt road this morning in the bright spring sunshine. There is a wide wet meadow beside the Yellow Breeches Creek. The meadow grass is already high and some of it is in head. There were pink asters on long stems and sunny yellow asters, too. Canada geese were feeding in the meadow, honking and squawking like a city traffic jam.

I walked home through our woods and stopped at the pond. For a moment, I saw one of the painted turtles sunning itself on a log. It slipped into the water as I approached. The air vibrated with the growling moan of a bullfrog. I looked for tracks along the edge of the pond. There is a narrow trail worn by the deer, which was covered with their hoof prints. And there were bird tracks at the water's edge. But the most interesting set of tracks were raccoon tracks—both adult-size and little-raccoon size! Now I know that we have baby raccoons around.

Two years ago, I was walking on the same road that I enjoyed this morning. As I rounded a curve in the road, I surprised four little raccoons without their mother. They were the size of large puppies and romping together the way puppies do. I stood still, watching them with delight. When they saw me, all of the little masked faces were startled, but each raccoon reacted differently. One loped away crying; one stared curiously; one slowly backed away; and one little animal growled fiercely. One of the most fascinating things about all of nature is that every individual—every masked raccoon, every stem of meadow grass, every yellow butterfly, every faraway star, every child—is unique in the universe.

© Trickle Creek Books

# A Track Trap

You might not always see an animal when you hike in the woods or fields, but you can usually find animal tracks. Look carefully when you pass a mud hole, a stream or pond, a brush pile, the entrance to an animal's den, or any animal path.

You can make a Track Trap by wetting and smoothing an area at the edge of a pond or creek. Check the area every morning for tracks. Or make another kind of Track Trap by filling a shallow box with dirt or sand that will hold a track. Bait the Track Trap with leftover food, peanut butter, or sunflower seeds, and place it near shrubs and bushes. Check it each morning. Use a field guide to tracks to help you identify the animals that visited during the night.

A permanent way to "trap a track" is to make a plaster cast of the track. You will need a container of plaster of Paris, a container of water, a strip of cardboard, a paper clip, and a plastic bag. When you find a good track, clean the track and the area around it with some dried grass. Bend the cardboard into a round collar and press it into the ground around the track. Secure it with a paper clip. Mix the plaster and water until they are creamy. Then slowly pour the plaster into the track and the collar around it. Let the plaster harden for about half an hour. Then you can dig up the cast and take it home in a plastic bag. When the plaster is completely hard, remove the cardboard collar and clean the cast with an old toothbrush. Don't forget to label the cast with the name of the animal that made the track and information about where you found it.

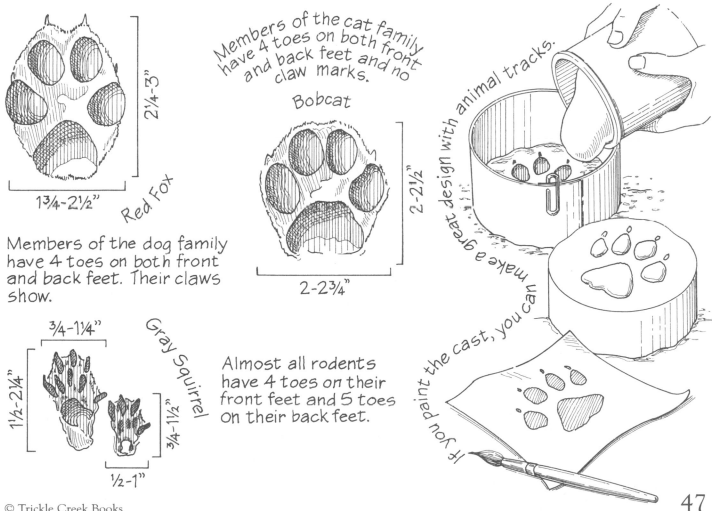

2¼-3"

1¾-2½"

Red Fox

Members of the dog family have 4 toes on both front and back feet. Their claws show.

Members of the cat family have 4 toes on both front and back feet and no claw marks.

Bobcat

2-2½"

2-2¾"

¾-1¼"

1½-2¼"

Gray Squirrel

¾-1½"

½-1"

Almost all rodents have 4 toes on their front feet and 5 toes on their back feet.

If you paint the cast, you can make a great design with animal tracks.

© Trickle Creek Books

# Spring EcoJournal

_____

_____

_____

_____

_____

_____

_____

_____

_____

_____

*May 27:* My father, who lives in Texas, often visits us in May when Pennsylvania is at its best—and when the morel mushrooms can be found. My father has studied mushrooms as a hobby all his life. He has collected them all over the world. Morels are one of his favorites because they are delicious to eat. They are strange-looking mushrooms, sometimes six or seven inches high, which look like upside down cones made of Swiss cheese.

Last year in late May, Bob and I found two morels at Trickle Creek. To save them for my dad, we froze one and dried one (just by leaving it on the counter top and forgetting to move it). When my father arrived yesterday, he thawed the frozen mushroom and soaked the dried mushroom in water. This morning he plucked some oyster mushrooms off a dying tree and added them to the two morels for our breakfast. He fried the mushrooms in butter, added some flour and milk to make a gravy, and then we ate them on toast. Hmm! Scrumptious!

After breakfast, we took a long walk. We didn't find any morels, but that's all right. My father knows a *secret place* in the southern part of the county where he can usually find them. We enjoyed the flowers and birds. The mayapples have little "apples" now, the blackberry blossoms are open, the dame's rockets are showier than ever. The towhees and mockingbirds are back from their winter homes in the South. We saw deer everywhere. It was a wonderful spring walk—with my dad.

© Trickle Creek Books

# Little Gardens in Containers

It's fun to create miniature gardens in small containers. It's so easy and manageable. Begin by putting a layer of gravel in the bottom of your container to provide drainage. Then add soil and plants. Try making a tiny woodland garden with moss, little ferns, tiny wildflowers, and other plants from the woods. Add a dried shelf mushroom or an interesting stone.

A hollow stump can be a wonderful planter. Fill it with rich soil, and plant wildflowers in it. Your stump will probably be a good home for mushrooms and insects, too.

You can even grow some fruits and vegetables in containers. If you plant strawberry plants, you will be able to pick berries—and eat them—by late spring.

Almost anything can be a container for plants.

Choose something interesting.

I've made these little gardens all my life!

A rotting stump produces food and breeding areas for insects and mushrooms.

Strawberries are a spring delight!

© Trickle Creek Books

# Spring EcoJournal

_____

_____

_____

_____

_____

_____

_____

_____

_____

_____

_____

_____

_____

_____

_____

_____

_____

_____

**May 30:** Bob got hit by a wren today. We've been watching a family of wrens in a birdhouse off the end of our deck. The family has been growing. Growing noisier—the little birds make a loud racket when their parents approach with insects for dinner. And growing bigger—the baby wrens are pushing their fluffy, feathered heads out of the entrance hole.

This morning when Bob saw a little wren hanging out of the birdhouse, he called me. "The baby wrens are ready to fly. If you want to see them take off, you'd better get out here!" I pushed Bailey into the house and came running just in time to see a funny embrace. Bob was standing in front of the birdhouse, about fifteen feet away from it. When the first baby bird took its courage in hand, it zoomed out of the entrance hole—straight into Bob's chest! Without thinking, he caught the bird in his hands, the way you would catch a ball that was speeding toward you. The wren's flight to Bob was so direct that it reminded me of a little child running into its father's arms, crying, "Daddy!" I think I saw the wren and the man who loves wrens look each other in the eye before Bob released the little bird, which wobbled into a shrub.

© Trickle Creek Books

# Oh, Those Baby Birds

When birds begin to build a nest in a birdhouse, you will have a perfect opportunity to observe them. Watch carefully to see who builds the nest. Is it only the male, or do the male and female work together? What materials do they carry to the nest and where are they gathering the materials?

Many birds that nest in birdhouses will let you come near if you are quiet and gentle. When the female bird has left the nest for awhile, you can use a mirror to look in the birdhouse and see the tiny eggs that have been laid there. Don't try to open the hinged roof of the birdhouse and don't disturb the house in any way. Look carefully—count the eggs and notice how the nest is made—but look quickly. Then quietly leave. Continue to check the nest every day or so. You can keep a record in your eco-journal of how many days pass before the baby birds hatch, what they look like, how long before their eyes open, how they grow and change, and when they leave the nest. If you are always respectful and careful when you peek inside the birdhouse, the parent birds may even feed the babies while you sit nearby. Listen for the racket of hungry little birds when their parents bring food.

If you see a little bird that is fully feathered on the ground, watch to see if it can hop or flutter to shelter in a shrub. If not, you can gently place it in a shrub. Its parents will probably continue to feed it there. If the baby bird is truly helpless or injured, call a veterinarian or your local Humane Society or animal shelter. They can often put you in touch with a wildlife rehabilitator who will know how to care for the bird. If you find a nest of baby birds that has toppled from a tree, carefully put the nest back into the tree that you think it fell from or put the nest in an empty margarine tub and attach it to a limb with wire. The parent birds will probably feed the babies there. The more you watch birds, the more you will see that they are wonderful parents.

Gently replace a nest that has fallen. The parent birds will still care for their young.

Use a mirror to peek in a birdhouse without disturbing it.

Never touch a baby bird unless you're sure it needs help.

© Trickle Creek Books

# Spring EcoJournal

_____

_____

_____

_____

_____

_____

_____

_____

_____

_____

_____

*May 31:* What better way to celebrate a spring day than to have a picnic? Bob and I packed our lunch—ham sandwiches on thick brown bread, sweet dark strawberries, a hunk of cheese, two brownies, and a box of dog biscuits. We walked to the pond on a lace carpet of fallen white petals. A high wind this morning blew the locust blossoms down in a fragrant shower. Abercrombie was excited about our taking a walk and carrying *food*. There was much digging and strutting and kicking up dirt. Bailey walked with us too, but at a proper "cat distance."

We spread a blanket on the grass beside the pond. Abercrombie begged for brownies, but he settled for dog biscuits wrapped in cheese. After awhile, he left to explore a groundhog hole. Bob and I ate in the spring sunshine and talked a little and grew drowsy. I squinted through half-closed eyes at the deep pink buds on the wild rose. The wind still sighed in the tops of the trees. Trickle Creek sang and laughed as it entered the pond.

I dreamed of baby squirrels, of birdsongs and frog songs, of a turtle with red eyes coming out of the mud, of the Carolina wren calling to its mate. I dreamed of Feisty sitting on my shoulder, of bluebird eggs like tiny blue grapes, of a baby rabbit cuddled in my hands. I dreamed of Bob catching a wren on its first flight and of the plud, plud of a crazy cardinal. I dreamed of spring things and smiled in my sleep.

© Trickle Creek Books

# Celebrate Spring

Climb up a tree that is flowering.

Stand still and feel the sun on your arms.

Listen to a breeze or a brook.

Roll down a grassy hill.

Follow a butterfly as far as you can.

Pick a bunch of wildflowers for a friend.

© Trickle Creek Books

# Directions for Making a Flower Press

To make a flower press, cut two 10¾-inch squares out of ⅜-inch plywood. Clamp the two pieces together and drill a 3/16-inch hole in each corner. Place the holes ¾ inch from the sides. Open up the holes in the *top* square to 5/16 inch. Carefully sand the squares, rounding the corners as you sand. Then apply two coats of varnish. (You can decorate the flower press by gluing a photograph of wildflowers or a design made with pressed flowers to the top square before applying the varnish.)

To assemble the flower press, you will need two fully threaded ¼-inch bolts with washers and wing-nuts. The bolts should be 6 to 8 inches long. Before inserting the bolts into the bottom square, add a little super glue to keep them permanently in place. The holes in the bottom square are smaller than those in the top square; it will be a tight fit, but the bolts can be screwed in.

Cut a number of 9-by-10-inch rectangles of newspaper and double-walled corrugated cardboard. Make a stack of flower press "sandwiches." Each sandwich is made of two pieces of cardboard filled with ten pieces of newspaper and two tissues in the center. (The flowers that you want to press are placed between the tissues.) To use the flower press, place the cardboard sandwiches on top of the bottom square of the press. Then put the top square on top of the sandwiches and tighten the wing-nuts over the washers to hold everything in place.

After you have arranged the flowers you want to press inside the flower press, tighten the wing-nuts a little more every day for a week. Keep the flower press in a warm dry place for two to six weeks. Check the flowers after a couple of weeks to see how they are drying. (*See page 33, "Pressed Memories," for ideas about what to do with pressed flowers.*)

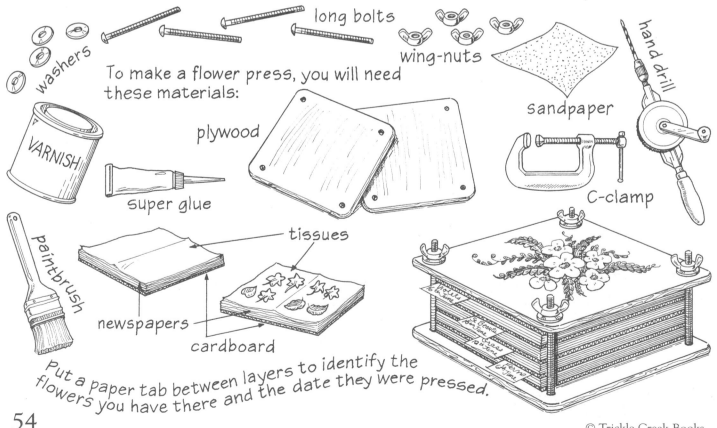

washers · long bolts · wing-nuts · sandpaper · hand drill

To make a flower press, you will need these materials:

VARNISH · plywood · C-clamp

super glue

paintbrush · newspapers · cardboard · tissues

Put a paper tab between layers to identify the flowers you have there and the date they were pressed.

54

© Trickle Creek Books

# Nest Box Requirements

Look at the chart below and find the bird or mammal you want to attract. Then as you build a nest box, use the dimensions given for each part of the box. (*See page 35, "Birdhouse Basics," for information on how to build a birdhouse or nest box.*)

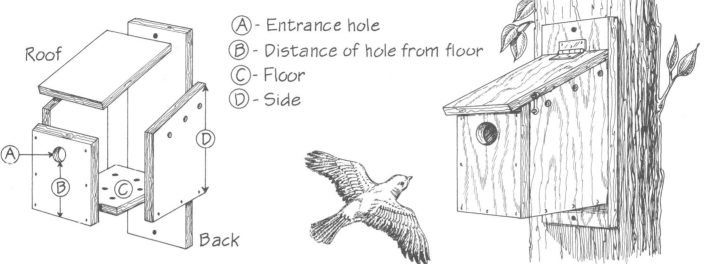

A - Entrance hole
B - Distance of hole from floor
C - Floor
D - Side

| ANIMAL | A - DIAMETER OF HOLE (INCHES) | B - DISTANCE OF HOLE FROM FLOOR (INCHES) | C - SIZE OF FLOOR (INCHES) | D - LENGTH OF SIDE (INCHES) | PLACEMENT OF BOX ABOVE GROUND (FEET) |
|---|---|---|---|---|---|
| **BIRDS** | | | | | |
| American Robin | none | none | 6x8 | 8 | 6-15 |
| Carolina Wren | 1½ | 1-6 | 4x4 | 6-8 | 6-10 |
| Eastern Bluebird | 1½ | 6 | 5x5 | 8 | 5-10 |
| House Finch | 2 | 4 | 6x6 | 6 | 6-12 |
| House Wren | 1-1¼ | 1-6 | 4x4 | 6-8 | 6-10 |
| Red-Headed Woodpecker | 2 | 10 | 6x6 | 12-15 | 12-20 |
| Screech Owl | 3 | 9-12 | 8x8 | 12-15 | 10-30 |
| Song Sparrow | none | none | 6x6 | 6 | 1-3 |
| Tufted Titmouse | 1¼ | 6-8 | 4x4 | 8-10 | 6-15 |
| White-Breasted Nuthatch | 1¼ | 6-8 | 4x4 | 8-10 | 12-20 |
| Wood Duck | 4 | 12-16 | 10x18 | 10-24 | 10-20 |
| **MAMMAL** | | | | | |
| Gray Squirrel | 3 | 11 | 8x9½ | 16 | 20-30 |

© Trickle Creek Books

# An EcoJournal for Every Season

*You'll want to own all four of them.*

Trickle Creek Books offers a series of four EcoJournals, one for each season, which are written by Toni Albert and illustrated by Margaret Brandt. All of the EcoJournals invite kids to explore the seasons with unusual nature activities and then to write about their experiences. The books include exquisitely illustrated writing pages for children, short entries from the author's nature journals that reflect her irrepressible delight in the natural world, and dozens of nature activities for children to try. Kids learn to develop a deep love and respect for the environment.

Here are some of the activities that are found in the other EcoJournals:

### A Kid's Summer EcoJournal

- Build a turtle platform
- Grow a birdhouse
- Make a mushroom spore print
- Attract moths with a "shining sheet"
- Create a sun print
- Make a creek aquarium

### A Kid's Fall EcoJournal

- Collect leaf galls and raise the larvae
- Build a bat house
- Collect a spider web
- Dissect an owl pellet
- Make leaf prints
- Sprout an acorn
- Take a sock walk

### A Kid's Winter EcoJournal

- Track animals in the snow
- Test the purity of snow
- Make an owl call
- Make woodpecker pizza and bird biscuits
- Make winter potpourri
- Make a snowman for the birds

Each EcoJournal sells for $9.95. Order from your bookseller, on-line bookseller, or directly from us.

## Trickle Creek Books

500 Andersontown Road
Mechanicsburg, PA   17055-6055

**Toll-free 24-hour telephone** - 800-353-2791
**Telephone** - 717-766-2638 • **Fax** - 717-766-1343
**Web sit**e - www.TrickleCreekBooks.com • **E-mail** - tonialbert@aol.com

**Satisfaction Guarantee** - If you are not satisfied with your purchase for any reason, return books for full refund. Thanks for ordering!

© Trickle Creek Books